food
for friends

Penny Stephens

SIMON &
SCHUSTER

LONDON · NEW YORK · SYDNEY · TORONTO

First published in Great Britain by
Simon & Schuster UK Ltd, 2008
A CBS Company
Copyright © 2008, Weight Watchers International, Inc.
Simon & Schuster UK Ltd, Africa House,
64-78 Kingsway, London WC2B 6AH

Weight Watchers, *POINTS* and **Core Plan** are trademarks of
Weight Watchers International Inc., and are used under its
control by Weight Watchers (UK) Ltd.

Weight Watchers Publications Team: Jane Griffiths,
Donna Watts, Nina Bhogal, Nina McKerlie and Eileen
Thornton
Photography by Steve Lee
Styling by Rachel Jukes
Food preparation and styling by Kim Morphew
Design and typesetting by Fiona Andreanelli
Printed and bound in China

A CIP catalogue for this book is available from the British
Library

ISBN 978-1-84737-300-7

1 3 5 7 9 10 8 6 4 2

Pictured on the front cover: Mini filo pastries, page 58.
Pictured on the back cover left to right: Roast turkey with
cranberry stuffing, page 56; Gourmet beef burger, page 38;
Pavlova with roasted vanilla plums, page 74.
Pictured on the inside front flap: Mocha chestnut tart,
page 76.
Pictured on the introduction: Roasted butternut squash and
Feta salad, page 24
Pictured on the Easy Brunches and Lazy Lunches chapter
opener: Orange maple syrup pancakes, page 12.
Pictured on the Suppers for Sharing chapter opener:
Meatballs with Moroccan rice, page 40.
Pictured on the High Days and Holidays chapter opener:
Sausages on sticks, page 52.
Pictured on the Sweet Sensations chapter opener: Pavlova
with roasted vanilla plums, page 74.

POINTS® value logo: You'll find this easy to read
POINTS value logo on every recipe throughout this
book. The logo represents the number of *POINTS* values per
serving each recipe contains. The easy to use *POINTS* Plan
is designed to help you eat what you want when you want
– as long as you stay within your daily *POINTS* allowance –
giving you the freedom to enjoy the food you love.

You'll find this distinctive **Core Plan**™ logo on every
recipe that can be followed freely on the **Core Plan**.
These recipes contain only foods that form part of the
Core Plan.

This symbol denotes a vegetarian recipe and assumes
that, where relevant, free range eggs, vegetarian cheese,
vegetarian virtually fat free fromage frais and vegetarian
low fat crème fraîche are used. Virtually fat free fromage
frais and low fat crème fraîche may contain traces of
gelatine so they are not always vegetarian. Please check
the labels.

This symbol denotes a dish that can be frozen.

Recipe notes:

Egg size: Medium, unless otherwise stated.
All fruits and vegetables: Medium sized, unless otherwise
stated.
Raw eggs: Only the freshest eggs should be used. Pregnant
women, the elderly and children should avoid recipes with
eggs that are not fully cooked or raw.
Recipe timings: These are approximate and meant to be
guidelines. Please note that the preparation time includes
all the steps up to and following the main cooking time(s).
Low fat polyunsaturated margarine: Use brands such as
Flora Light, St Ivel Gold and Benecol Light.

Core Plan: If following the **Core Plan** you have a limited
allowance of 2 teaspoons of healthy oil a day (olive,
sunflower, safflower, flaxseed, rapeseed) to use in recipes
as you choose.

Contents

Whether you are entertaining friends or having a family dinner, there's no need to put your weight loss on hold. *Food for Friends* is the ideal cookbook to get your weight loss off to a flying start. And it fits perfectly when you are following the KickStart programme, as many of the recipes complement the menus in the KickStart booklet.

The four chapters cover food right through the day and for many occasions. You'll find a selection of ***POINTS* Plan** and **Core Plan** recipes, as well as a great choice of meat, fish and vegetarian food.

The chapter on Easy Brunches and Lazy Lunches has a selection of quick and light meals that can be enjoyed from morning to noon, or in fact all day. There are recipes that can be prepared ahead and others that can be put together at the last minute. Suppers for Sharing is exactly what it says – food to be prepared simply and enjoyed with friends and family. It covers traditional recipes such as Coq au Vin through to a modern Potato and Leek Pie with shortcrust pastry. High Days and Holidays will give you some great ideas on how to keep your weight loss on track, whether you are looking for a delicious Bonfire Night supper or a New Year celebration meal.

Last but not least is Sweet Sensations, a wonderfully tempting choice of puddings, all with low ***POINTS*** values. They are easy recipes to end a meal or satisfy a sweet tooth.

Food for Friends is a great collection that you will come to treasure and return to time after time. Enjoy!

Easy Brunches and Lazy Lunches

Weekends are the perfect time to enjoy a late, satisfying breakfast or a quick and easy lunch. In this chapter you'll find a great selection of delicious recipes that you can serve up for family or friends and still keep your weight loss on track. Choose between Egg and Bacon Poppets or Orange Maple Syrup Pancakes for an easy brunch or, for a lazy lunch, the Courgette Pots with Tomato Sauce or Roasted Butternut Squash and Feta Salad. For something more filling try the one-pot Sunday Chicken. Enjoy

Bacon and Rocket Risotto

Total **POINTS** values per recipe **20½** Calories per serving **205**
Takes 35 minutes Serves **6**

Adding low fat soft cheese helps create the creamy consistency normally associated with traditional risotto rice, but lacking with brown rice.

low fat cooking spray
2 onions, sliced
3 garlic cloves, crushed
250 g (9 oz) easy cook brown rice
4 rashers smoked lean back bacon, chopped
2 litres (3½ pints) hot chicken or vegetable stock
75 g (2¾ oz) low fat soft cheese with onion and garlic
110 g (4 oz) rocket leaves
freshly ground black pepper

1 Spray a large non stick frying pan with low fat cooking spray and heat until hot. Add the onions and stir fry for 3 minutes, then add the garlic and continue cooking for another 2 minutes. Add the rice and chopped bacon and stir to coat.

2 Pour in the stock a ladleful at a time, stirring occasionally and allowing it to be absorbed before adding more. Once all the stock has been added and the rice is tender, remove from the heat and stir in the soft cheese. Taste and season with freshly ground black pepper. Stir through most of the rocket, reserving a few leaves for garnish before serving.

Variation You can exchange the rocket for watercress as an alternative, for the same **POINTS** values.

Smoky Fish Patties

Total **POINTS** values per recipe **10½** Calories per serving **191**
Takes 20 minutes to prepare, 15–20 minutes to cook
Serves **4** ❄

*These delicious patties are easy to make and can be served with a zero **POINTS** value green salad for lunch or on their own for a great brunch.*

600 g (1 lb 5 oz) potatoes, peeled and chopped
350 g (12 oz) smoked haddock fillets, skinned
1 bay leaf
8 spring onions, chopped finely
4 tablespoons finely chopped fresh parsley
low fat cooking spray
freshly ground black pepper

1 Bring a large pan of water to the boil, add the potatoes and simmer for 15–20 minutes until tender. Drain them well and mash.

2 Meanwhile, place the haddock in a wide, shallow, lidded non stick frying pan and pour over enough water to just cover. Add the bay leaf, bring to the boil then reduce the heat, cover and simmer for 5 minutes until the fish flakes. Drain the fish, remove the bay leaf and leave to cool slightly.

3 Flake the haddock and add to the mash with the spring onions and parsley. Season with freshly ground black pepper (the fish will probably make the mixture salty enough).

4 Shape the mixture into eight patties. Spray a non stick frying pan with low fat cooking spray and heat until hot. Add the patties and fry for 5 minutes, turning once, until golden and hot in the middle. You may need to do this in batches. Serve two patties each.

Tip To freeze, shape into patties and then open freeze before wrapping in clingfilm and packing into a freezerproof container.

Oven Baked Tomatoes and Eggs

Total *POINTS* values per recipe **12** + Calories per serving **227** + Takes 15 minutes to prepare, 35 minutes to cook + Serves **4** ♥

An easy and satisfying brunch to share with friends.

low fat cooking spray
600 g (1 lb 5 oz) potatoes, peeled and diced
8 tomatoes, halved
4 sprigs of fresh thyme
4 eggs
freshly ground black pepper
2 tablespoons snipped fresh chives, to serve

1 Preheat the oven to Gas Mark 6/200°C/fan oven 180°C. Spray a small, non stick roasting tin with low fat cooking spray. Add the potatoes and stir, then spray again to thoroughly coat. Bake for 20 minutes, then stir before adding the tomatoes and thyme sprigs. Roast for a further 15 minutes until the potatoes are tender and the tomatoes are beginning to char. Season with freshly ground black pepper.

2 Meanwhile, bring a shallow lidded pan of water to the boil, reduce the heat to a steady simmer and break the eggs into the water one at a time. Cover the pan and cook for 3 minutes. Remove the eggs with a slotted spoon.

3 Serve the potatoes and tomatoes on warmed plates with a poached egg on top. Sprinkle with the chives.

Variation If you prefer, use 20 small vine tomatoes to share between four, instead of eight tomatoes, roasting them on the vine. The *POINTS* values will remain the same.

Egg and Bacon Poppets

Total *POINTS* values per recipe **22½** + Calories per serving **158** + Takes 5 minutes to prepare, 15 minutes to cook + Serves **8**

Pop these out of the muffin tin for a different way of serving eggs and bacon.

low fat cooking spray
8 medium slices wholemeal bread, crusts removed and each slice cut into four triangles
8 eggs
2 rashers lean back bacon, chopped
freshly ground black pepper

1 Preheat the oven to Gas Mark 4/180°C/fan oven 160°C. Spray eight holes of a muffin tin with low fat cooking spray.

2 Arrange four bread triangles in each hole, pressing down to cover the bottom and sides with the points sticking out. Crack an egg into the middle of each and divide the chopped bacon between the holes, scattering over each egg.

3 Bake for 15 minutes until golden and the egg white is set. Season with freshly ground black pepper and serve.

Variation For a vegetarian option, use the same amount of Quorn Deli Bacon Style Rashers, instead of the bacon, for a *POINTS* value of 2½ per serving.

Orange Maple Syrup Pancakes

Total **POINTS** values per recipe **22½** + Calories per serving **213** + Takes 20 minutes + 10 minutes resting + Serves **8** 🅥

Maple syrup has a fantastically strong flavour, so even if you dilute it with orange juice you still get that lovely sugary hit coming through.

225 g (8 oz) self raising flour
2 tablespoons caster sugar
2 eggs
300 ml (10 fl oz) skimmed milk
4 oranges
6 tablespoons maple syrup

1 Place the flour and sugar in a large bowl and mix well. Make a well in the middle. Crack the eggs into the well and stir, allowing them to draw in the flour. Once it is too thick to mix, begin adding the milk gradually to form a smooth batter. Set aside for 10 minutes.

2 Finely grate the zest from the oranges and cut the pith away. Carefully cut between the segments, holding the fruit over a bowl to collect any juice. Once the segments have been removed, squeeze the remaining pith to extract any juice.

3 Stir the orange zest into the batter. Heat a smooth non stick griddle pan or frying pan until hot. Add spoonfuls of the batter mixture to the pan, cook for 1–2 minutes until bubbles rise to the surface and then turn and cook for a further 1 minute until golden and puffed up. Remove and keep warm. Continue with the rest of the mixture to make 24 pancakes.

4 Meanwhile, place the maple syrup in a small pan. Add the orange segments and juice. Place on a low heat for 1–2 minutes, stirring occasionally until warm. Divide the pancakes between eight plates, three pancakes each, and drizzle over the syrup and orange segments. Serve immediately.

Crunchy Nectarine Yogurt Pots

Total **POINTS** values per recipe **15½** + Calories per serving **198** + Takes 10 minutes + cooling + Serves **4** 🅥

This is a healthy start to the day or could be served as a refreshing dessert at the end of a meal.

4 ripe nectarines or peaches, stoned and quartered
2 pieces pared lemon rind
4 tablespoons honey
300 g (10½ oz) 0% fat Greek yogurt
4 tablespoons granola, such as Crunchy Sultana and Honey Oat Cereal

1 Place the nectarines or peaches in a small lidded pan with the lemon rind and pour over 200 ml (7 fl oz) water. Bring to the boil, cover and simmer for 5 minutes until the fruit is just soft. Drizzle over the honey and set aside to cool completely.

2 Take four serving glasses, place two pieces of fruit in the base of each and cover with 2 heaped tablespoons of the yogurt then ½ tablespoon of granola. Repeat, ending with the granola.

Tip Poached fruit will keep covered in the fridge for up to 3 days.

Variation You could try this with eight small or four large plums, instead of the nectarines, as an alternative. The **POINTS** values will remain the same.

Easy Scotch Broth

Total **POINTS** values per recipe **16½** + Calories per serving **185** + Takes 15 minutes to prepare, 45 minutes to cook + Serves **6** ❄

Traditional Scotch broth is a lamb stew that is cooked on the stove for days. This version is more straightforward and yet still delicious.

2 litres (3½ pints) chicken stock
110 g (4 oz) pearl barley, washed
300 g (10½ oz) carrots, peeled and cut into sticks
225 g (8 oz) swede, peeled and diced
3 celery sticks, chopped
450 g (1 lb) lean lamb steaks, cut into strips
bouquet garni of 1 bay leaf, 1 sprig of fresh
    rosemary and 1 sprig of fresh thyme,
    tied together
150 g (5½ oz) Savoy cabbage, shredded
salt and freshly ground black pepper

1   In a large lidded pan, bring the stock to the boil. Add the barley, carrots, swede, celery, lamb and bouquet garni. Cover and simmer for 45 minutes until the barley is tender.

2   Stir in the cabbage and simmer for 1–2 minutes until just wilted. Remove the bouquet garni, season and serve hot in shallow bowls.

Serving Suggestion Serve with 700 g (1 lb 9 oz) potatoes, boiled in their skins, for an extra 1½ **POINTS** values per serving.

Avocado and Grapefruit Salad

Total **POINTS** values per recipe **13** + Calories per serving **212** + Takes 10 minutes + Serves **4** ♥

Serve this zingy salad to friends as a light and refreshing lunch.

4 pink grapefruits
2 small avocados
finely grated zest of a lime
1 teaspoon finely chopped fresh red chilli
8 fresh mint leaves, shredded
2 teaspoons artificial sweetener (optional)

1   Cut the skin and pith from the grapefruits using a serrated knife. Carefully cut between the segments holding the fruit over a bowl to collect any juice. Once the segments have been removed, squeeze the remaining pith to extract any juice.

2   Halve each avocado, remove the stones and then peel off the skins. Slice into wedges, arrange on four plates and spoon over the grapefruit segments.

3   Mix together the grapefruit juice, lime zest, chilli and mint. Taste and add sweetener if required. Drizzle over the fruit and serve immediately.

Tip Try to buy pink grapefruit as they are naturally sweeter than the white variety so you'll need less sweetener.

Aubergine, Spring Onion and Spinach Salad

Total **POINTS** values per recipe **0** + Calories per serving **55** + Takes 25 minutes + Serves **4** ❤

This is a warm salad with an Asian style dressing.

2 small aubergines
2 red peppers, de-seeded and cut into bite-size pieces
4 tablespoons light soy sauce
4 teaspoons finely grated ginger
2 teaspoons finely chopped fresh red chilli
1 teaspoon artificial sweetener
a bunch of spring onions, cut into long thin strips
4 handfuls of spinach leaves
2 tablespoons chopped fresh coriander, to garnish

1 Trim the ends from the aubergines and then cut long thin slices down the length. A vegetable peeler is good for this. Cut each slice in half across its width.

2 Heat a ridged griddle pan or non stick frying pan until hot. Place the aubergine slices and pepper pieces in the pan and cook for 2–3 minutes, turning once, until charred. Remove from the pan and keep warm. You will have to do this in batches.

3 In a small pan, place the soy sauce, ginger, chilli, sweetener and 3 tablespoons of water and bring to the boil. Add the spring onions and cook for 1–2 minutes until just wilted. Add the aubergines and peppers.

4 Divide the spinach between four plates and top with the aubergine and pepper mixture. Drizzle over any remaining dressing and garnish with the coriander before serving.

Serving suggestion Serve with 150 g (5½ oz) cooked wholewheat pasta per person, for an extra **POINTS** value of 2 per serving.

Courgette Pots with Tomato Sauce

Total **POINTS** values per recipe **7½** + Calories per serving **142** + Takes 30 minutes to prepare, 20–30 minutes to cook + Serves **4** ❤

low fat cooking spray
450 g (1 lb) courgettes, grated
1 sprig of fresh rosemary, leaves chopped
2 eggs
1 x 200 g tub low fat soft cheese with garlic and herbs
salt and freshly ground black pepper

For the sauce:
2 shallots, peeled and diced finely
20 cherry tomatoes, halved
1 tablespoon tomato purée

1 Preheat the oven to Gas Mark 3/160°C/fan oven 140°C. Base line four ovenproof ramekins with non stick baking parchment and lightly spray with low fat cooking spray.

2 Spray a large non stick frying pan with low fat cooking spray and add the courgettes and rosemary. Cook over a low heat, stirring, for 5–7 minutes until beginning to brown and any liquid has evaporated. Set aside to cool slightly.

3 Beat together the eggs and soft cheese in a bowl, then stir into the courgettes. Season and spoon into the ramekins. Place the ramekins in a roasting tin and pour in boiling water to come two thirds of the way up the sides of the ramekins. Bake for 20–30 minutes until set and just golden on top.

4 Meanwhile, make the sauce. Spray a small pan with low fat cooking spray and heat until hot. Add the shallots and stir fry for 3–4 minutes. Add the tomatoes and cook for 5 minutes with 4 tablespoons of water until mushy. Stir in the tomato purée and season with freshly ground black pepper.

5 To serve, remove the courgette pots from the tin and tip out using an extra plate so that they are cooked side up. Remember to remove the baking parchment. Spoon over the sauce before serving.

Curried Beef Skewers with Yogurt Dip

Total *POINTS* values per recipe **19½** + Calories per serving **322** + Takes 25 minutes to prepare + marinating and soaking + Serves **4**

Marinating the beef in yogurt and spices not only adds flavour but tenderises the meat too.

2 tablespoons medium curry powder
300 g (10½ oz) 0% fat Greek yogurt
400 g (14 oz) beef escalope, cut into 1 cm (½ inch) thin strips
175 g (6 oz) dried couscous
200 ml (7 fl oz) boiling water, to cover
2 red peppers, de-seeded and cut into pieces
75 g (2¾ oz) frozen peas, defrosted
finely grated zest and juice of a lemon
2 garlic cloves, crushed
10 cm (4 inch) piece cucumber, de-seeded and chopped finely
3 tablespoons fresh mint, chopped
freshly ground black pepper

1 Place the curry powder in a small non stick pan and heat until hot. Stir for 1 minute before adding 2 tablespoons of water. Remove from the heat and cool.

2 Add 4 tablespoons of the yogurt to the curry paste. Mix together, add the beef, cover and leave to marinate at room temperature for 20 minutes.

3 Meanwhile, place the couscous in a bowl and pour over enough boiling water to just cover. Set aside to soak.

4 Preheat the grill to medium. Thread the beef on to metal skewers and grill for 10 minutes, turning regularly, until beginning to char.

5 Fluff the couscous up with a folk and stir in the peppers, peas, lemon zest and juice. Season with freshly ground black pepper.

6 Mix together the remaining yogurt with the garlic, cucumber and mint. Serve the skewers on a mound of couscous with a dollop of the yogurt on the side.

Variation You can try this recipe using the same weight of skinless boneless chicken breast, in place of the beef, for a *POINTS* value of 4½ per serving.

Tip You can use wooden skewers rather than metal ones, but make sure you soak them in water for 5 minutes before using to help prevent them from burning.

Sunday Chicken

Total **POINTS** values per recipe **51½** + Calories per serving **270** + Takes 10 minutes to prepare, 50 minutes to cook + Serves **8**

This is a great one-pot Sunday roast.

low fat cooking spray
8 x 75 g (2¾ oz) skinless chicken thigh fillets
8 x 75 g (2¾ oz) skinless chicken drumsticks
4 leeks, trimmed and sliced thinly
2 lemons, cut into quarters
4 sprigs of fresh rosemary
850 ml (1½ pints) hot chicken stock
600 g (1 lb 5 oz) potatoes, peeled and diced
450 g (1 lb) parsnips, peeled and diced
salt and freshly ground black pepper

1 Preheat the oven to Gas Mark 6/200°C/fan oven 180°C. Spray a large non stick frying pan with low fat cooking spray and heat until hot. Add all the chicken and cook for 2–3 minutes, turning until each piece is brown all over. You may have to do this in batches. Remove from the heat.

2 Place the leeks in the bottom of a large roasting tin or divide between two smaller tins. Top with the chicken and any pan juices, lemon quarters and rosemary. Pour over the stock. Scatter over the potatoes and parsnips and spray liberally with low fat cooking spray. Season. Roast for 40–50 minutes until the chicken and vegetables are tender. When a skewer is inserted into a drumstick the juices should run clear. Serve immediately.

Serving suggestion Serve with steamed broccoli and carrots, for no additional **POINTS** values.

Variation Swap the parsnips for the same quantity of peeled and diced sweet potato for a change. The **POINTS** values will remain the same.

Peppery Pesto Pasta

Total **POINTS** values per recipe **19** + Calories per serving **311** + Takes 15 minutes + Serves **4** ✔

This is a quick home made pesto that is flavourful and really easy to make.

250 g (9 oz) spaghetti
2 tablespoons pine nut kernels
30 g (1¼ oz) rocket
1 tablespoon extra virgin olive oil
1 garlic clove, chopped roughly
10 g (¼ oz) Parmesan cheese, grated finely
salt and freshly ground black pepper

1 Bring a large pan of water to the boil, add the spaghetti and cook according to the packet instructions.

2 Meanwhile, gently brown the pine nut kernels in a non stick pan until they are golden all over.

3 Place the rocket, olive oil, garlic and 1 tablespoon of water in a food processor (or use a hand blender) and blitz until a rough paste forms. Add the pine nut kernels and blend so that they form the pesto. Season.

4 Drain the pasta, reserving 2 tablespoons of the cooking liquid. Return to the pan with the reserved liquid, add the pesto and toss until well combined. Serve hot, sprinkled with the Parmesan cheese.

Tip The pesto will keep covered in the fridge for up to 5 days.

Chicken Liver Pâté with Melba Toast

Total **POINTS** values per recipe **14** + Calories per serving **140** + Takes 20 minutes + 30 minutes chilling + Serves **6**

Pâté is quick and easy to make and this version keeps the **POINTS** values low.

25 g (1 oz) low fat polyunsaturated margarine
2 banana shallots, peeled and chopped
1 garlic clove, chopped
350 g (12 oz) chicken livers, rinsed and dried on kitchen paper
1½ tablespoons tomato purée
1½ tablespoons brandy
6 slices medium white bread, crusts removed

1 Melt the margarine in a small pan and, when hot, add the shallots. Cook, stirring, for 3–4 minutes. Add the garlic and continue cooking for another 2 minutes until softened. Add the chicken livers and sauté for 5 minutes. Stir in the tomato purée and brandy.

2 Remove from the heat and cool slightly. Transfer to a food processor or use a hand blender and blend until smooth. Spoon into six individual small ramekins or serving dishes and, when cool, cover and chill for 30 minutes.

3 To make the melba toast, preheat the grill to medium. Cut through each piece of bread horizontally to make two slices. Cut each of these into two triangles and then toast under the grill on one side. Serve warm with the pâté.

Tip You can make the pâté up to 24 hours in advance, cover and chill until required.

Chicken Mulligatawny Soup

Total **POINTS** values per recipe **12** + Calories per serving **145** + Takes 15 minutes to prepare, 20 minutes to cook + Serves **8**
❄

This is a filling and warming stew-like soup, that is great for winter days.

low fat cooking spray
2 large onions, diced
4 carrots, peeled and diced
300 g (10½ oz) skinless boneless chicken breast, sliced thinly
4 garlic cloves, chopped
2 tablespoons mild curry powder
2 tablespoons tomato purée
2 tablespoons smooth mango chutney
3 litres (5¼ pints) hot chicken stock
125 g (4½ oz) basmati rice

1 Spray a large lidded saucepan with low fat cooking spray and heat until hot. Add the onions and carrots and cook, stirring for 3 minutes until just tender. Add the chicken and garlic and continue cooking for 2 minutes.

2 Stir in the curry powder, tomato purée and mango chutney. Cook for 1 minute then add the stock and rice. Bring to the boil, cover and simmer for 20 minutes until the vegetables are tender and the rice is cooked.

3 Serve the soup in warm bowls.

Tip This is a great soup for 210 g (7¼ oz) leftover cooked chicken with skin removed. Just slice it thinly and add for the last 3–4 minutes of cooking to warm through. The **POINTS** values will remain the same.

Smoked Trout Filo Quiches

Total **POINTS** values per recipe 17 + Calories per serving **175** + Takes 10 minutes to prepare, 30 minutes to cook + Serves **6**

Smoked trout makes a very tasty quiche and these individual ones are particularly attractive to serve for lunch.

low fat cooking spray
10 spring onions, chopped
6 x 15 g sheets filo pastry
100 g (3½ oz) smoked trout, cut into strips
5 eggs, beaten
150 g (5½ oz) low fat soft cheese
3 tablespoons chopped fresh parsley
freshly ground black pepper
a zero **POINTS** value mixed salad, to serve

1 Preheat the oven to Gas Mark 4/180°C/fan oven 160°C.

2 Spray a small non stick frying pan with low fat cooking spray and heat until hot. Add the spring onions and stir fry for 2–3 minutes until softened. Remove from the heat and cool slightly.

3 Spray six 10 cm (4 inch) individual loose-bottomed tins (see tip) with low fat cooking spray. Working quickly so that the filo pastry does not dry out too much, cut each sheet in four to make four rectangles. Spray with low fat cooking spray and line each tin with four rectangles of pastry, scrunching the edges so that they don't hang over too far.

4 Divide the trout between the tins. Beat together the eggs and soft cheese with three quarters of the parsley. Season with freshly ground black pepper and pour into the pastry cases. Bake for 25–30 minutes until set and golden. Serve the quiches warm, garnished with the remaining parsley, and with the salad on the side.

Tip If you don't have individual tins, use a Yorkshire pudding tray with 10 cm (4 inch) holes and, once cooked, carefully loosen the quiches and slide out.

Roasted Butternut Squash and Feta Salad

Total **POINTS** values per recipe 10½ + Calories per serving **191** + Takes 15 minutes to prepare, 30 minutes to cook + Serves **6** ♥

A delicious and colourful salad, that combines the heat of chilli and the tang of Greek cheese with the sweetness of warm roasted vegetables.

700 g (1 lb 9 oz) butternut squash, peeled, de-seeded and cut into chunks
6 beetroots, trimmed and quartered
8 whole garlic cloves, unpeeled
low fat cooking spray
1 tablespoon chilli flakes
2 tablespoons pumpkin seeds
1 x 200 g bag mixed salad leaves
110 g (4 oz) reduced fat Feta cheese, crumbled

For the dressing:
2 tablespoons extra virgin olive oil
2 tablespoons balsamic vinegar

1 Preheat the oven to Gas Mark 6/200°C/fan oven 180°C. Place the butternut squash, beetroot and garlic in a roasting tin and spray with low fat cooking spray. Sprinkle over the chilli flakes and roast for 30 minutes, turning occasionally, until the vegetables are softened and charred at the edges.

2 Meanwhile, brown the pumpkin seeds by dry frying them in a non stick frying pan, moving them around the pan for 2–3 minutes until they just change colour and begin popping. Set aside.

3 Remove the squash and beetroot from the oven and leave to cool slightly. Remove the garlic cloves from the tin.

4 For the dressing, pop the garlic cloves from their skins (they should slide out easily) and mash the flesh with the olive oil and vinegar.

5 To serve, arrange the salad leaves on serving plates, top with the butternut squash and beetroot and crumble over the Feta. Sprinkle over the pumpkin seeds and the salad dressing.

Suppers for Sharing

Everyone will enjoy the simple, delicious recipes in this chapter, whatever the occasion. Whether its easy entertaining you are looking for or something to satisfy that 'fast food craving' there are plenty of mouth-watering meals to choose from. You'll easily impress with Meatballs with Moroccan Rice, Hungarian Pork with Peppers or the Gourmet Beef Burger There's plenty to choose from.

Baked Egg and Potatoes with Thyme

Total *POINTS* values per recipe **20½** ✤ Calories per serving **384** ✤ Takes 25 minutes to prepare, 15–20 minutes to cook ✤ Serves **4** ♥

A simple yet delicious supper dish that is great for informal entertaining.

low fat cooking spray
800 g (1 lb 11 oz) potatoes, peeled and cut into long, thin chips
2 onions, sliced
850 ml (1½ pints) vegetable stock
3 tablespoons fresh thyme leaves
110 g (4 oz) low fat soft cheese with garlic and herbs
4 eggs
8 Quorn Deli Bacon Style Rashers
freshly ground black pepper

1 Preheat the oven to Gas Mark 6/200°C/fan oven 180°C.

2 Spray a large non stick frying pan with low fat cooking spray and heat until hot. Add the potatoes and onions and cook over a medium heat, stirring regularly for 5 minutes until beginning to brown. Add the stock and thyme and continue cooking for 5–10 minutes until softened.

3 Remove from the heat and stir in the soft cheese. Season with freshly ground black pepper. Spoon the mixture into four ovenproof gratin dishes (see tip), making a well in the middle of each dish. Crack an egg into each well and bake for 15–20 minutes until golden and the egg is set.

4 Meanwhile, preheat the grill to medium. Grill the rashers for 2–3 minutes until golden. Serve the rashers on top of the baked potatoes and eggs.

Tip If you don't have individual gratin dishes, bake in one dish, making four wells for the eggs and spoon out to serve four people.

Warm Balsamic Pears with Bacon

Total *POINTS* values per recipe **6½** ✤ Calories per serving **134** ✤ Takes 20 minutes ✤ Serves **4**

This makes a great dinner party starter, or serve two pears and a rasher of bacon per person with a large zero *POINTS* value salad for a lunch for two, for a *POINTS* value of 3½ per serving.

4 whole pears, peeled and cored
3 tablespoons balsamic vinegar
1 teaspoon artificial sweetener
1 star anise
1 piece pared lemon rind
2 rashers lean back bacon
a handful of rocket leaves, to serve

1 Lay the pears in a lidded saucepan so that they fit snugly. Mix together the balsamic vinegar and sweetener with 150 ml (5 fl oz) water and pour over the pears. Add the star anise and lemon rind, cover and bring slowly to a simmer. Cook for 10 minutes until the pears are just tender. You may need to turn them so that they get an even colour. When cooked, remove from the heat, carefully take out the pears and set aside. Bring the juice back to the boil and simmer uncovered for 2–3 minutes to reduce.

2 Meanwhile, preheat the grill to high and cook the bacon until crispy. Cut into small strips.

3 To serve, slice the pears, place on a plate, drizzle over the juices and scatter with the bacon. Garnish with rocket.

Variation For an interesting dessert, omit the bacon and rocket, cool the pears, cover and chill. Serve with a 60 g (2 oz) scoop of low fat ice cream and the juice drizzled over. The *POINTS* values will be 2 per serving.

Sweet and Spicy Crab Cakes

(3) POINTS VALUE

Total **POINTS** values per recipe 11½ ✤ Calories per serving 226 ✤ Takes 15 minutes to prepare + chilling time, 10–15 minutes to cook ✤ Serves 4 ❄ (crab cakes only)

This is a really colourful dish, which would be lovely served al fresco with a large zero **POINTS** value green salad.

700 g (1 lb 9 oz) sweet potato, peeled and cut into
    chunks
2 garlic cloves, peeled
2 x 170 g cans white crab meat in brine or water
1 fresh red chilli, de-seeded and diced
3 tablespoons chopped fresh coriander
finely grated zest of 2 limes
low fat cooking spray
freshly ground black pepper

For the salsa:
4 vine tomatoes, de-seeded and diced
10 cm (4 inch) piece cucumber, de-seeded and
    diced
4 spring onions, sliced
juice of 2 limes plus extra lime wedges, to serve

1 Bring a large lidded pan of water to the boil and add the sweet potato and garlic. Cover and simmer for 10–15 minutes until tender. Drain thoroughly, return to the pan and place over a low heat for 30 seconds to allow any excess water to evaporate. Mash, squashing the garlic in with the potatoes, and leave until cool enough to handle.

2 Drain the crab meat and stir into the mash with the chilli, coriander and lime zest. Season with freshly ground pepper. Shape the mixture into four cakes and place on a plate in the fridge for 30 minutes.

3 Meanwhile, to make the salsa, combine all the ingredients (except the lime wedges), cover and chill.

4 Spray a non stick frying pan with low fat cooking spray and heat until hot. Cook the cakes for 3–5 minutes until golden and hot, turning once. Serve with a dollop of salsa and the lime wedges.

Olive and Lemon Lamb Chops

(7½) POINTS VALUE

Total **POINTS** values per recipe 29 ✤ Calories per serving 387 ✤ Takes 5 minutes to prepare + 20 minutes marinating, 20 minutes to cook ✤ Serves 4

This is a quick and easy dinner party dish.

8 x 75 g (2¾ oz) lean lamb chops, well trimmed
finely grated zest and juice of a lemon
½ teaspoon chilli flakes
30 g (1¼ oz) pitted black olives in brine, drained
    and diced
2 tomatoes, de-seeded and diced
low fat cooking spray
salt and freshly ground black pepper

1 Season the lamb chops and place in a non-metallic ovenproof dish. Mix together the lemon zest, juice and chilli flakes and drizzle over the meat. Leave to marinate at room temperature for 20 minutes (see tip).

2 Preheat the oven to Gas Mark 5/190°C/fan oven 170°C. Scatter the olives and diced tomatoes over the lamb, spray everything with low fat cooking spray and bake for 20 minutes until the meat is cooked through.

3 Serve the lamb with the olive and tomato topping and juices spooned over.

Tip If marinating the chops for longer (up to 24 hours), cover with clingfilm and refrigerate.

Serving suggestion Serve with 100 g (3½ oz) new potatoes per person and steamed green beans, for an additional **POINTS** value of 1 per serving.

Hungarian Pork with Peppers

 ✓ (6 POINTS VALUE)

Total **POINTS** values per recipe 48½ + Calories per serving **620** + Takes 20 minutes to prepare, 15 minutes to cook + Serves **8**

The smoked paprika and green peppers give a Hungarian flavour to this braised pork dish.

8 x 150 g (5½ oz) lean pork chops
4 teaspoons smoked paprika
low fat cooking spray
4 onions, sliced
4 garlic cloves, sliced
4 green peppers, de-seeded and sliced
500 ml (18 fl oz) chicken stock
400 g (14 oz) brown rice
225 g (8 oz) frozen peas
salt and freshly ground black pepper

1 Season the chops on both sides and dust with the paprika. Spray a large lidded non stick frying pan (see tip) with low fat cooking spray and heat until hot. Add the chops and cook for 5 minutes, turning until golden. You may have to do this in batches. Remove from the pan and set aside.

2 Re-spray the pan and add the onions, garlic and peppers. Stir fry for 3–4 minutes until beginning to soften. Reduce the heat, add the stock and return the chops to the pan on top of the peppers and onions. Bring to the boil, reduce to a simmer, cover and cook for 15 minutes until the chops are cooked through.

3 Meanwhile, bring a large pan of water to the boil, add the rice, return to the boil and simmer according to the packet instructions. Add the peas for the last 2 minutes of the cooking time. Drain well.

4 Serve the chops on top of the rice and peas with the peppers, onions and juices.

Tip If you don't have a large lidded non stick frying pan, use a baking sheet to cover your pan, making sure you check the liquid doesn't evaporate too much.

Spicy Chickpea Patties

✓ (2 POINTS VALUE)

Total **POINTS** values per recipe 8½ + Calories per serving **150** + Takes 10 minutes + Serves **4** ♥

These delicious little patties are similar to falafel.

2 teaspoons cumin seeds
2 teaspoons coriander seeds
2 x 400 g cans chickpeas, drained
4 spring onions, chopped
1 tablespoon chopped fresh red chilli
2 egg whites
low fat cooking spray

1 Lightly crush the cumin and coriander seeds in a mortar and pestle (see tip). Place the chickpeas in a food processor or use a hand blender and roughly blend. Add the seeds, spring onions, chilli and egg whites and pulse a couple of times until blended.

2 Divide the mixture into eight and shape into patties. Spray a non stick frying pan with low fat cooking spray and heat until hot. Add the patties and cook for 4–5 minutes, turning occasionally until golden. Take care when turning them as they are quite fragile. Serve two warm patties each.

Tip If you don't have a mortar and pestle, use the end of a rolling pin to crush the seeds in a small bowl.

Serving suggestion Serve with a large mixed salad of lettuce, cucumber, cherry tomatoes and red pepper, for no additional **POINTS** values.

Lamb Steaks with Oven Roasted Tomatoes

Total *POINTS* values per recipe 32 + Calories per serving 384
+ Takes 10 minutes to prepare, 40 minutes to cook + Serves 6

The flavour of tomatoes is intensified and sweetened with a little balsamic vinegar, which goes particularly well with lamb.

6 x 225 g (8 oz) baking potatoes
6 beef steak tomatoes, sliced thickly
6 tablespoons balsamic vinegar
6 x 125 g (4½ oz) lean lamb leg steaks
3 sprigs of fresh rosemary
low fat cooking spray
salt and freshly ground black pepper

To serve:
6 handfuls of rocket leaves
3 tablespoons fat free dressing

1 Preheat the oven to Gas Mark 5/190°C/fan oven 170°C. Place the potatoes on a tray and bake for 40 minutes until cooked through.

2 Meanwhile, arrange the tomato slices in an ovenproof dish, drizzle over the vinegar and season with freshly ground black pepper. Bake for 30 minutes on the rack above the potatoes.

3 Season the lamb steaks on both sides. Roughly chop the rosemary and press into the lamb. Spray a non stick frying pan with low fat cooking spray and heat until hot. Add the lamb and cook for 5 minutes, turning occasionally until golden and cooked to your liking.

4 Serve the lamb with the jacket potatoes, tomato slices and any juices, and the rocket drizzled with the dressing.

Variation You could use a mixed bag of salad leaves instead of the rocket if preferred. The *POINTS* values will remain the same.

Fillet Steak with Mustard Wedges

Total *POINTS* values per recipe 25 + Calories per serving 357 +
+ Takes 15–20 minutes to prepare, 30 minutes to cook + Serves 4

This is a low *POINTS* value version of the classic steak, chips and peas and makes a lovely celebration dinner.

500 g (1 lb 2 oz) potatoes, cut into thin wedges
low fat cooking spray
2 tablespoons wholegrain mustard
4 x 150 g (5½ oz) fillet steaks
110 g (4 oz) frozen peas
4 tablespoons 0% fat Greek yogurt
4 teaspoons horseradish sauce
salt and freshly ground black pepper

1 Preheat the oven to Gas Mark 6/200°C/fan oven 180°C. Place the potato wedges on a roasting tray and spray with low fat cooking spray. Mix the mustard with 2 teaspoons of water and drizzle over the wedges, tossing them to coat thoroughly. Bake for 30 minutes, turning occasionally, until golden and cooked through.

2 Meanwhile, spray a non stick frying pan or griddle pan with low fat cooking spray and heat until hot. Season the steaks and cook for 5 minutes for medium (8–10 minutes for well done), turning occasionally until browned and firm to the touch.

3 Bring a small pan of water to the boil, add the peas and simmer for 2 minutes. Drain.

4 Mix together the yogurt and horseradish and serve with the wedges, steak and peas.

Serving suggestion Serve the steak and wedges with steamed green beans instead of the peas, for a *POINTS* value of 6 per serving.

Cheesy Aubergine Rolls

Total **POINTS** values per recipe **9** ✤ Calories per serving **91** ✤ Takes 25 minutes to prepare, 20–25 minutes to cook ✤ Serves **4** ✿

Softened and lightly charred strips of aubergine are rolled around a tasty mixture of cheese, basil and pesto.

1 large aubergine
low fat cooking spray
60 g (2 oz) light soft mozzarella, diced
2 tomatoes, de-seeded and diced
30 g (1¼ oz) pitted black olives in brine, drained and chopped
1 tablespoon tomato pesto
12 basil leaves
25 g (1 oz) fresh white breadcrumbs
15 g (½ oz) Parmesan cheese, grated
a zero **POINTS** value green salad, to serve

1 Heat a griddle pan or non stick frying pan until hot. Trim the ends from the aubergine and then slice thinly down its length to get approximately 12 slices. Spray each slice with low fat cooking spray on both sides. Place in the pan and cook until charred and softened, turning once. You may have to do this in batches. Remove and set aside.

2 Meanwhile, preheat the oven to Gas Mark 4/180°C/fan oven 160°C. In a bowl, mix together the mozzarella, tomatoes, olives and pesto. Lay one basil leaf in the middle of an aubergine slice, top with a dollop of the mozzarella mixture, roll up and place seam side down in an shallow ovenproof dish. Repeat with the rest of the slices.

3 Mix together the breadcrumbs and Parmesan and sprinkle over the rolls. Bake for 20–25 minutes until the breadcrumbs are golden. Serve three rolls each with the salad.

Variation To make this a vegan recipe, omit both the mozzarella and Parmesan cheeses and instead add 3 tablespoons pine nut kernels to the filling in step 2. The **POINTS** values will remain the same.

Stilton Mushroom Filo Parcels

Total **POINTS** values per recipe **25½** ✤ Calories per serving **212** ✤ Takes 20 minutes to prepare + 30 minutes to cook ✤ Serves **6** ✿

Try serving these delicious filo parcels with a zero **POINTS** value green salad.

low fat cooking spray
750 g (1 lb 10 oz) mixed mushrooms, chopped finely
6 spring onions, sliced
3 sprigs of fresh thyme, leaves only
2 garlic cloves, crushed
150 g (5½ oz) Stilton cheese, crumbled
12 x 15 g sheets filo pastry
freshly ground black pepper
2 teaspoons caraway seeds (optional)

1 Preheat the oven to Gas Mark 6/200°C/fan oven 180°C.

2 Spray a non stick frying pan with low fat cooking spray and heat until hot. Add the mushrooms, spring onions, thyme and garlic and cook over a high heat for 5–7 minutes. The mushrooms should release their juices, which will then evaporate. Remove from the heat.

3 Crumble in the cheese and mix to combine. Season with freshly ground black pepper (the Stilton will make the mixture salty enough).

4 Lay a sheet of pastry on a board, spray with low fat cooking spray and top with another sheet. Spoon a sixth of the mixture into the middle, fold over two opposites sides of pastry and roll up to make a parcel. Spray with low fat cooking spray and sprinkle with the caraway seeds (if using). Repeat to make six parcels. Place on a non stick baking tray and bake for 20–25 minutes until golden.

Variation If you don't like blue cheese, try using the same amount of Cheddar instead, for a **POINTS** value of 4 per serving.

Chicken and Lentils with Wine and Herbs

Total **POINTS** values per recipe 56 ✛ Calories per serving **418** ✛ Takes 20 minutes to prepare, 25 minutes to cook ✛ Serves **8**

Puy lentils are small and dark green and have a delicious flavour, particularly when cooked with wine and herbs.

8 sprigs of fresh thyme
8 x 150 g (5½ oz) skinless boneless chicken breasts
8 rashers lean back bacon
low fat cooking spray
2 red onions, sliced
4 garlic cloves, crushed
4 celery sticks, chopped
4 carrots, peeled and diced
300 g (10½ oz) Puy lentils
1.2 litres (2 pints) chicken stock
300 ml (10 fl oz) white wine
2 sprigs of fresh rosemary
800 g (1 lb 11 oz) potatoes, peeled and chopped
4 tablespoons chopped fresh parsley, to garnish

1 Preheat the oven to Gas Mark 6/200°C/fan oven 180°C. Place a sprig of thyme on each chicken breast, wrap a bacon rasher around each one and place them in a roasting tin. Spray with low fat cooking spray and bake for 20 minutes until golden and cooked through. (Insert a skewer and the juices should run clear. If not, return to the oven for another 5 minutes.)

2 Meanwhile, spray a lidded saucepan with low fat cooking spray and heat until hot. Add the onions, garlic, celery and carrots with 2 tablespoons of water and cook for 3–4 minutes, stirring, until just softened. Add the lentils, stock, wine and rosemary. Bring to the boil, cover and simmer for 20 minutes or until the lentils are tender. Add a little water if the mixture becomes too dry. Remove the rosemary.

3 Meanwhile, bring a saucepan of water to the boil, add the potatoes and cook for 15–20 minutes. Drain and mash.

4 Serve the chicken on a bed of lentils with a dollop of mash. Garnish with the parsley.

Gourmet Beef Burger

Total **POINTS** values per recipe 30 ✛ Calories per serving **246** ✛ Takes 25 minutes to prepare + chilling ✛ Serves **6**

Sometimes you just fancy something yummy – well here it is in lean form but with all the flavour and juiciness.

600 g (1 lb 5 oz) lean minced steak
1 tablespoon dried thyme or mixed herbs
low fat cooking spray
2 onions, sliced thinly
salt and freshly ground black pepper

To serve:
a handful of lettuce leaves
3 x 60 g (2 oz) crusty rolls, halved
6 tablespoons tomato relish

1 Place the mince in a bowl with the thyme or mixed herbs and season. Mix well and shape into six large burgers, squeezing the mixture together with your hands. Transfer to a plate and chill for 10 minutes.

2 Spray a medium non stick frying pan with low fat cooking spray and heat until hot. Add the onions and cook over a medium to high heat for 5–10 minutes until golden and crispy. You may need to add a tablespoon or two of water to prevent them from sticking. Remove from the pan and keep warm.

3 Respray the pan with low fat cooking spray and heat until hot. Add the burgers and cook for 10 minutes, turning occasionally, until browned and cooked through.

4 To serve, place a lettuce leaf on each half roll, add a burger, top with a tablespoon of the relish and finally add the crispy onions. Serve immediately.

Variation You can also use the same amount of lamb mince, instead of steak mince to make the burgers, for a **POINTS** value of 6 per serving.

Meatballs with Moroccan Rice

Total *POINTS* values per recipe **38½** ✦ Calories per serving **363** ✦ Takes 30 minutes to prepare, 45 minutes to cook ✦ Serves **6**

a large pinch of saffron
2 tablespoons of boiling water
low fat cooking spray
2 onions, diced
3 garlic cloves, crushed
600 g (1 lb 5 oz) lean minced beef
1 tablespoon mixed dried herbs
325 g (11½ oz) basmati rice
3 carrots, peeled and chopped
3 cardamom pods
2 teaspoons coriander seeds, crushed lightly
2 teaspoons cumin seeds, crushed lightly
1 cinnamon stick
2 bay leaves
finely grated zest and juice of 1½ lemons
40 g (1½ oz) ready to eat dried apricots, chopped
1.5 litres (2¾ pints) vegetable stock
salt and freshly ground black pepper

1. Place the saffron in a small bowl and cover with 2 tablespoons boiling water. Set aside to infuse. Spray a non stick frying pan with low fat cooking spray and heat. Add the onions and stir fry for 3–4 minutes until soft. Add the garlic and cook for another 2 minutes. Remove from the heat.

2. Place the mince in a large bowl and mix in 3 tablespoons of the onion mixture and the mixed herbs. Season. Shape the mixture into 18 meatballs. Re-spray the frying pan with low fat cooking spray and heat until hot. Cook the meatballs, turning frequently, for 10 minutes until browned.

3. In a large lidded saucepan, place all the remaining ingredients including the saffron and its liquid and remaining onion mixture. Cover, bring to the boil and simmer for 30 minutes. Add the meatballs and continue cooking for 10–15 minutes until the rice is tender. To serve, divide the rice between warm plates and top with the meatballs.

Duck with Hoisin Noodles

Total *POINTS* values per recipe **32½** ✦ Calories per serving **479** ✦ Takes 20 minutes to prepare, 50 minutes to cook ✦ Serves **4**

This is a take on Crispy Duck with Pancakes, which uses noodles instead.

4 x 175 g (6 oz) skinless duck legs
2 x 125 g packets medium egg noodles
low fat cooking spray
12 baby corn, halved
a bunch of spring onions, shredded
4 tablespoons hoisin sauce
2 tablespoons fresh coriander, chopped
half a small cucumber, cut into thin sticks

1. Bring a large lidded pan of water to the boil, add the duck legs, cover and simmer for 50 minutes. Drain well and pat dry with kitchen paper. Preheat the grill to medium and grill the legs for 3–4 minutes, turning once. This will give a better colour to the meat and some lovely crispy bits.

2. Meanwhile, bring a large saucepan of water to the boil, add the noodles and cook according to the packet instructions. Drain well and set aside.

3. Spray the same pan with low fat cooking spray and heat until hot. Add the baby corn and stir fry for 2 minutes, then add the spring onions and continue cooking for another minute. Add the hoisin sauce, 150 ml (5 fl oz) water and the noodles and warm through gently, then stir in the coriander.

4. To serve, pull the duck meat from the bone and shred it; it should come away easily. Divide the noodles and sweetcorn between four warm bowls, top with the duck meat and cucumber sticks.

Potato and Leek Pie

Coq au Vin

Total **POINTS** values per recipe **29** + Calories per serving **343** + Takes 20 minutes to prepare, 30–40 minutes to cook + Serves **4** ❶ ❄

This is a pastry tart filled with lightly caramelised leeks and topped with thin and crispy potatoes.

low fat cooking spray
3 large leeks, sliced thinly
2 garlic cloves, crushed
2 sprigs of fresh thyme
250 g (9 oz) ready made shortcrust pastry
175 g (6 oz) potatoes, peeled and sliced thinly
salt and freshly ground black pepper

1 Spray a large non stick frying pan with low fat cooking spray and heat until hot. Add the leeks and cook over a medium heat for 2–3 minutes. Reduce the heat, add the garlic and thyme with 2 tablespoons water and continue cooking for 10 minutes. The leeks should be very soft and slightly browned. Remove from the heat and season.

2 Preheat the oven to Gas Mark 6/200°C/fan oven 180°C. Roll out the pastry to approximately 28 x 22 cm (11 x 8½ in). Use a fork to mark the edges of the pastry to neaten it and place it on a baking sheet. Spread the leeks evenly over the pastry so that the fork markings create a border. Arrange the thinly sliced potatoes on top and spray with low fat cooking spray. Sprinkle with freshly ground black pepper. Bake for 30–40 minutes until the pastry and potatoes are golden and cooked. Serve the pie warm.

Variation Try making this pie with a mixture of leeks and onions using 2 leeks and 2 onions, cooking them together in step 1, for the same **POINTS** values.

Serving suggestion Serve with steamed broccoli and carrots, for no additional **POINTS** values.

Total **POINTS** values per recipe **39½** + Calories per serving **403** + Takes 25 minutes to prepare, 1 hour to cook + Serves **6** ❄ (casserole)

A rich wine-flavoured stew with both chicken breast and the tasty brown meat from drumsticks, this makes a great prepare-ahead supper for guests.

low fat cooking spray
3 x 165 g (5¾ oz) skinless boneless chicken breasts, cut in half
6 x 75 g (2¾ oz) skinless chicken drumsticks
3 celery sticks, chopped
12 baby onions, peeled
4 carrots, peeled and cut into chunks
2 tablespoons flour
300 ml (10 fl oz) chicken stock
300 ml (10 fl oz) white wine
bouquet garni of 1 bay leaf, 1 sprig of fresh rosemary and 1 sprig of fresh thyme, tied together
300 g (10½ oz) rice

1 Spray a large lidded ovenproof casserole with low fat cooking spray and heat until hot. Add the chicken breasts and drumsticks (you may have to do this in batches) and cook for 4–5 minutes, turning until brown all over. Remove from the pan and set aside.

2 Preheat the oven to Gas Mark 4/180°C/fan oven 160°C. Re-spray the casserole with low fat cooking spray, add the celery, onions and carrots and stir fry for 5 minutes until softened. Add the flour and cook for a further minute. Return the chicken to the pan with the stock, wine and bouquet garni and bring to the boil. Cover and cook in the oven for 1 hour.

3 Bring a saucepan of water to the boil, add the rice and cook according to packet instructions. Drain.

4 Remove the bouquet garni and serve the casserole with the rice.

Tip Prepare this ahead, cool and keep refrigerated for up to 2 days. To reheat, warm through on the hob until piping hot.

6 1/2
POINTS
VALUE ®

High Days and Holidays

Whether it's a casual get together on Bonfire Night or a family celebration at Christmas, this is a chapter that has it all. Everyone will love the Finger Licking Chicken and Sausages on Sticks while standing around the fire. Or for a drinks party, why not try the Mini Filo Pastries or serve up home made Blinis with Smoked Salmon? There is even a great Christmas Roast Turkey with Cranberry Stuffing, roast potatoes and gravy to keep you on track right the way through the year.

Sweet and Spicy Tomato Soup

 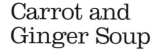

Total **POINTS** values per recipe **5** + Calories per serving **65** + Takes 10 minutes to prepare, 35 minutes to cook + Serves **6** ❤ ❄

This soup makes a great meal in a mug for Bonfire night.

750 g (1 lb 10 oz) large vine tomatoes, halved
2 red peppers, de-seeded and quartered
1 yellow pepper, de-seeded and quartered
3 red chillies
2 sprigs of fresh rosemary
low fat cooking spray
1.2 litres (2 pints) hot vegetable stock
freshly ground black pepper

To serve:
6 tablespoons low fat natural fromage frais
3 tablespoons snipped fresh chives

1 Preheat the oven to Gas mark 6/200°C/fan oven 180°C. Place the tomatoes, peppers, whole chillies and rosemary in a large roasting tin. Spray with low fat cooking spray and roast for 35 minutes until beginning to char. Transfer to a food processor or use a hand blender, add a little of the stock and blend until smooth. Sieve to remove any pips, pushing as much pulp through as possible and season with freshly ground black pepper.

2 Return the soup to the pan with the remaining stock and warm gently until hot. Serve each bowl with a dollop of fromage frais and some chives sprinkled on top.

Tip Although vine tomatoes are more expensive, they do retain more flavour and so enhance the soup.

Carrot and Ginger Soup

Total **POINTS** values per recipe **0** + Calories per serving **53** + Takes 10 minutes to prepare, 20 minutes to cook + Serves **6** ❤ ❄

This is an appropriate colour for Halloween and the ginger adds a great zing.

low fat cooking spray
2 onions, chopped
3 garlic cloves, chopped
500 g (1 lb 2 oz) carrots, peeled and chopped
6 cm (2½ in) piece root ginger, peeled and chopped
2 bay leaves
2.5 litres (4½ pints) hot vegetable stock

1 Spray a large lidded saucepan with low fat cooking spray and heat until hot. Add the onions and stir fry for 5 minutes, then stir in the garlic, carrots, ginger and bay leaves and cook for 1 more minute before adding the stock. Bring to the boil, cover and simmer for 20 minutes until tender.

2 Remove from the heat, take out the bay leaves and transfer to a food processor or use a hand blender in the pan. Blend until smooth (you may have to do this in batches). Return to the pan to heat through. Serve in warm bowls or in mugs.

Variation You can use the same amount of parsnips, in place of the carrots, for a **POINTS** value of 1 per serving.

Finger Licking Chicken

4 POINTS VALUE

Total *POINTS* values per recipe **30½** ✤ Calories per serving **145** ✤ Takes 5 minutes to prepare + 20 minutes marinating, 30 minutes to cook ✤ Serves **8** ❄

Wrap these in paper serviettes and they make great finger food for Bonfire night or a barbecue.

16 x 75 g (2¾ oz) skinless chicken drumsticks
6 tablespoons light soy sauce
finely grated zest and juice of a lime
2 teaspoons chilli flakes
2 teaspoons grated ginger
2 teaspoons tomato purée
2 teaspoons artificial sweetener

1 Place the drumsticks in an ovenproof non-metallic dish. Mix together the remaining ingredients and pour over the meat. Leave to marinate for 20 minutes.

2 Preheat the oven to Gas Mark 5/190°C/fan oven 170°C. Bake the chicken in the marinade for 30 minutes until golden and the juice runs clear when a skewer is inserted. Serve two chicken drumsticks each with the juices and marinade to dip into.

Variation Try this with 800 g (1 lb 11 oz) skinless boneless chicken breast in place of the drumsticks. Cut the chicken into strips and marinade as above. Thread on to 16 skewers and grill for 5-10 minutes until golden. The *POINTS* values will be 1½ per serving.

Mediterranean Baked Squash

3 POINTS VALUE

Total *POINTS* values per recipe **12½** ✤ Calories per serving **274** ✤ Takes 10 minutes to prepare, 1 hour 15 minutes to cook ✤ Serves **6** ❤

Butternut squash acts as a great container for a filling, and of course you can eat the whole thing, skin included.

850 ml (1½ pints) vegetable stock
200 g (7 oz) brown rice
3 x 600 g (1 lb 5 oz) butternut squash, cut in half and de-seeded
16 cherry tomatoes, quartered
125 g (4½ oz) black olives in brine, drained and halved
6 roasted peppers in brine, drained and chopped roughly
2 teaspoons dried thyme
4 tablespoons tomato purée
freshly ground black pepper

1 In a large lidded pan, bring the stock to the boil, then add the rice. Bring back to the boil, cover, reduce to a simmer and cook for 25 minutes until tender. Check occasionally, adding more water if boiling dry, so that almost all the stock has been absorbed by the end.

2 Meanwhile, preheat the oven to Gas Mark 4/ 180°C/fan oven 160°C. Place the squash skin side down in a large ovenproof dish. Pour 150 ml (5 fl oz) water in the bottom of the dish and bake for 20 minutes.

3 In a pan, mix together the cooked rice, tomatoes, olives, peppers, thyme and tomato purée. Season with freshly ground black pepper.

4 Remove the squash from the oven, spoon the rice mixture into the squash, cover with foil and bake for 40–50 minutes until the squash is tender. Remove from the pan and serve hot.

Serving suggestion Serve with a zero *POINTS* value mixed salad.

Veggie Jackets

Total **POINTS** values per recipe 17 + Calories per serving 172 + Takes 15 minutes to prepare, 30 minutes to cook + Serves 8 ✔

Jacket potatoes are synonymous with Bonfire Night. Topped with this veggie Bolognese, you have a quick meal.

4 x 225 g (8 oz) baking potatoes
low fat cooking spray
1 onion, chopped
1 red pepper, de-seeded and sliced
2 garlic cloves, chopped
150 g (5½ oz) closed cup mushrooms, sliced
2 x 400 g can chopped tomatoes
1 x 300 g packet frozen Quorn mince
1 vegetable stock cube, crumbled
2 teaspoons mixed herbs
2 tablespoons tomato purée
50 g (1¾ oz) reduced fat Cheddar cheese, grated, to serve

1 Preheat the oven to Gas Mark 5/190°C/fan oven 170°C. Place the potatoes on a baking sheet and bake for 45 minutes until tender.

2 Meanwhile, spray a large pan with low fat cooking spray and heat until hot. Add the onion and stir fry for 5 minutes until softened. Add the pepper, garlic and mushrooms and continue cooking for another 5 minutes. Stir in the tomatoes, Quorn mince, stock cube, herbs and tomato purée. Bring to the boil, reduce the heat and simmer for 20 minutes, stirring occasionally.

3 Serve the potatoes, one half each, smothered with the veggie mince and topped with the grated cheese.

Serving suggestion Serve with a salad of sliced tomatoes and cucumber dressed with 2 tablespoons of fat free salad dressing, for no additional **POINTS** values.

Sausage and Butterbean Hotpot

Total **POINTS** values per recipe 25 + Calories per serving 257 + Takes 20 minutes to prepare + cooling, 25 minutes to cook + Serves 8 ❄

This is a really quick and easy stew for feeding friends on Bonfire Night.

2 x 400 g packets Weight Watchers Premium Pork Sausages
low fat cooking spray
4 red peppers, de-seeded and chopped
4 carrots, peeled and chopped
2 x 400 g cans chopped tomatoes with garlic and herbs
2 x 198 g cans sweetcorn, drained
2 x 400 g cans butterbeans, drained
2 vegetable stock cubes, crumbled

1 Preheat the grill to medium. Grill the sausages for around 10 minutes, turning frequently until browned all over. Remove from the grill and, when cool enough to handle, chop into bite sized pieces.

2 Spray a large lidded pan with low fat cooking spray and heat until hot. Add the peppers and carrots and stir fry for 3–4 minutes. Add the tomatoes, sweetcorn, butterbeans and stock cubes with the sausage pieces and 450 ml (16 fl oz) water. Bring to the boil, cover and simmer for 25 minutes until the carrots are tender.

Vegetarian option To make a vegetarian version of this, use 12 x 42 g Quorn sausages in place of the pork sausages. Grill and cut into pieces and stir into the pan for the last 5 minutes of cooking time in step 2. The **POINTS** values will be 2 per serving.

Sausages on Sticks

Total *POINTS* values per recipe 49½ ✤ Calories per serving **348** ✤ Takes 15 minutes ✤ Serves **8**

Cook these on the bonfire or barbecue as they make for great outdoor eating.

16 thick low fat sausages such as Weight Watchers Premium Pork Sausages
16 streaky bacon rashers
8 tablespoons sweet chilli sauce, to serve

1 Preheat the grill to medium. Thread each sausage on to a skewer (see tip). Wrap a rasher of bacon around each one and grill for around 10 minutes until golden and cooked through.

2 Serve the sausages on skewers with the chilli sauce to dip into.

Tip Use metal skewers if cooking on a barbecue or fire but remember that the handles will get hot. If grilling, you can use wooden skewers but pre-soak them in water or cover the tips with foil to help prevent them from burning.

Variation If preferred, use the same amount of tomato ketchup, in place of the chilli sauce for dipping, for the same *POINTS* values per serving.

Vegetarian option Use the same amount of Quorn sausages and Quorn Deli Bacon Style Rashers, in place of the pork sausages and bacon, for a *POINTS* value of 3 per serving. Cut each Quorn sausage into four pieces and each rasher into three. Thread on to the skewers, alternating the sausage and rasher pieces. Spray with low fat cooking spray before grilling until golden and cooked through.

Celeriac Rosti with Creamy Roasted Vegetables

Total *POINTS* values per recipe 9½ ✤ Calories per serving **197** ✤ Takes 20 minutes to prepare, 40 minutes to cook ✤ Serves **6** ♥

Rosti make a delicious and low *POINTS* value base for lots of toppings.

3 yellow peppers, de-seeded and sliced
3 red onions, sliced
700 g (1 lb 9 oz) butternut squash, peeled, de-seeded and cut into chunks
12 garlic cloves, unpeeled
low fat cooking spray
500 g (1 lb 2 oz) celeriac, peeled and grated
500 g (1 lb 2 oz) Desiree potatoes, peeled and grated
150 g (5½ oz) low fat soft cheese with herbs
3 tablespoons chopped fresh curly parsley
salt and freshly ground black pepper

1 Preheat the oven to Gas Mark 6/200°C/fan oven 180°C. Place the peppers, onions, squash and garlic cloves in a large roasting dish. Spray with low fat cooking spray and cook for 40 minutes until tender and beginning to char.

2 Meanwhile, squeeze as much liquid as possible from the grated celeriac and potatoes and dry on kitchen paper. Mix the two together, season and divide into 12 balls. Spray a non stick frying pan with low fat cooking spray and heat until hot. Place a ball in the pan and flatten with the back of a spatula until very thin. Cook for 5–6 minutes, turning occasionally, until golden and cooked through. You may need to cook these in batches. Remove from the pan and keep warm.

3 Remove the roasting dish from the oven, take out the garlic cloves and squeeze out the soft flesh. Mix with the soft cheese and parsley then stir into the hot roasted vegetables with a little hot water – enough to make a creamy sauce.

4 Serve two rosti each on warm plates topped with the creamy roasted vegetables.

Turkey Stir Fry

Total **POINTS** values per recipe 30½ ✛ Calories per serving 268 ✛ Takes 20 minutes ✛ Serves **8**

A fast and nutritious way to use up any left over turkey.

low fat cooking spray
2 leeks, trimmed and sliced
2 red peppers, de-seeded and sliced
16 sprouts, trimmed and halved
16 baby corn
2 carrots, peeled and cut into thin sticks
300 g (10½ oz) beansprouts
500 g (1 lb 2 oz) cooked skinless brown and white turkey meat
100 ml (3½ fl oz) hot vegetable stock
2 tablespoons korma curry powder
4 x 200 g packets Amoy Straight to Wok Noodles
8 sprigs of fresh coriander, to garnish

1 Spray a wok or large non stick frying pan with low fat cooking spray and heat until hot. Add all the vegetables except the beansprouts and stir fry for 4–5 minutes until beginning to brown and soften slightly. Add the beansprouts and turkey and cook for a further 2 minutes.

2 Mix together the stock and curry powder and add to the wok along with the noodles. Stir over a high heat for 1–2 minutes until everything is piping hot. Serve immediately garnished with the coriander.

Variation This recipe works well with the same amount of leftover cooked chicken, in place of the turkey, for the same **POINTS** values.

Variation If you don't have left over turkey, you can use 600 g (1 lb 5 oz) uncooked turkey steaks. Cut into strips and brown for 5 minutes at the start before adding the vegetables. The **POINTS** values would remain the same.

Cranberry Duck

Total **POINTS** values per recipe 28 ✛ Calories per serving 459 ✛ Takes 20 minutes to prepare, 20 minutes to cook ✛ Serves **4**

Cranberries and orange both work well with duck and help to cut through the richness of the meat.

4 oranges, with finely grated zest from 2
low fat cooking spray
4 x 175 g (6 oz) skinless duck breasts
125 g (4½ oz) fresh or frozen cranberries
500 ml (18 fl oz) chicken stock
1 kg (2 lb 4 oz) parsnips, peeled and chopped
300 g (10½ oz) green beans, trimmed
2 teaspoons artificial sweetener
salt and freshly ground black pepper

1 Cut away the skin from all the oranges and then segment, collecting any juice. Set aside.

2 Spray a lidded non stick frying pan with low fat cooking spray and heat until hot. Add the duck breasts and sear on both sides, cooking for 3–4 minutes until brown. Add the orange zest, segments and juice with the cranberries and chicken stock. Bring to the boil, cover and simmer for 20 minutes.

3 Meanwhile, bring a pan of water to the boil, add the parsnips and cook for 15 minutes until tender. Drain and mash well, adding a little seasoning to taste.

4 Remove the duck breasts from the pan and keep warm. Bring a pan of water to the boil, add the beans and cook for 3–5 minutes until just tender. Drain well.

5 Meanwhile, bring the sauce to the boil, squashing the cranberries to release their juices, and simmer for 1 minute until reduced and slightly thickened. Stir in the sweetener and taste, adding more if required.

6 Serve the duck sliced with the parsnip mash, green beans and the sauce drizzled over.

Roast Turkey with Cranberry Stuffing

Total **POINTS** values per recipe **33** + Calories per serving **287** +
Takes 1¼ hours to prepare, 2 hours to cook + resting + Serves **6**

Christmas lunch can be a very balanced meal. This recipe shows you how to keep the **POINTS** values low and still enjoy a delicious meal.

1 x 2.5 kg (5 lb 8 oz) turkey, giblets removed
half a lemon

For the stuffing:
110 g (4 oz) couscous
200 ml (7 fl oz) hot chicken stock
low fat cooking spray
1 onion, diced
75 g (2¾ oz) fresh or frozen cranberries
finely grated zest of a lemon
2 tablespoons chopped mixed fresh herbs, e.g.
    parsley, thyme, sage
1 egg, beaten

For the roast potatoes:
600 g (1 lb 5 oz) potatoes, peeled and chopped
2 sprigs of fresh rosemary

For the sprouts:
1 x 500 g packet Brussels sprouts, trimmed
3 lean back bacon rashers, chopped

To serve:
4 heaped teaspoons (14 g total weight) chicken
    gravy granules
300 ml (10 fl oz) boiling water

1 Preheat the oven to Gas Mark 4/180°C/fan oven 160°C. To make the stuffing, place the couscous in a large bowl and pour over the hot stock. Leave to soak for 10 minutes.

2 Meanwhile, spray a small non stick frying pan with low fat cooking spray and heat until hot. Add the onion and stir fry over a low heat for 10 minutes until softened, adding a little water if it gets too dry. Add the cranberries and cook for 5 minutes until the skins have burst. Set aside to cool slightly.

3 Fluff up the couscous and stir in the onion and cranberry mixture with the lemon zest, herbs and egg. The mixture should be slightly sticky.

4 Fill the neck cavity of the turkey with half the stuffing, pulling the skin down and over the bulge. Tuck it in securely underneath. Place the remaining stuffing in a 450 g (1 lb) loaf tin lined with non stick baking parchment and bake with the turkey for the last 30 minutes. Weigh the turkey and place in a roasting tin. Place the half lemon inside the other end of the turkey and spray with low fat cooking spray. Roast for 2 hours (20 minutes per 500 g plus an extra 20 minutes). Test that the turkey is cooked by sticking a skewer into the thickest part and seeing if the juices run clear.

5 Meanwhile, for the potatoes, bring a pan of water to the boil, add the potatoes and simmer for 5 minutes. Drain well. Place in a large roasting tin and spray liberally with low fat cooking spray. Scatter over the rosemary and roast above the turkey for 45 minutes, turning occasionally until golden.

6 For the sprouts, bring a pan of water to the boil, add the sprouts and cook for 3–4 minutes until just tender. Drain. Spray a small non stick frying pan with low fat cooking spray and heat until hot. Add the bacon pieces and cook for 2 minutes, stirring, before adding the sprouts. Stir fry for 2–3 minutes until beginning to brown. Keep warm.

7 Remove the turkey from the oven and allow to rest for 10 minutes before carving. Make up the gravy with boiling water following the packet instructions.

8 To serve, remove the skin from the turkey, carve thinly and serve two slices (50 g /1¾ oz per slice) each with one sixth of the stuffing, potatoes and sprouts and the gravy poured over.

Tip Don't forget there are plenty of zero **POINTS** value vegetables you can serve with this meal – try carrots, green beans, cabbage, broccoli and cauliflower.

Blinis with Smoked Salmon

Total **POINTS** values per recipe **10** ✤ Calories per serving **58** ✤ Takes 20 minutes ✤ Serves **12** (3 each) ❄ (blinis only)

Buckwheat flour has a slightly nutty flavour that complements the smoked salmon deliciously.

100 g (3½ oz) buckwheat flour
½ teaspoon baking powder
1 egg, beaten
175 ml (6 fl oz) skimmed milk
low fat cooking spray

For the topping:
75 g (2¾ oz) smoked salmon, cut into pieces
6 tablespoons fat free natural fromage frais
1 tablespoon chopped fresh dill, plus sprigs to garnish
freshly ground black pepper
2 tablespoons mock caviar (optional)

1 Place the buckwheat flour and baking powder in a bowl and mix well. Make a well in the middle. Add the egg and begin mixing, gradually drawing in the buckwheat flour until it becomes too thick to mix. Add a little milk and continue mixing and adding until you have a thick batter. Beat well.

2 Spray a smooth griddle pan or non stick frying pan with low fat cooking spray and heat until hot. Add tablespoons of the batter to the griddle or pan and cook for 1–2 minutes until bubbles appear on the surface. Flip them over and cook for another minute until golden on both sides. Remove from the pan and repeat to make 36 pancakes.

3 To serve, top each blini with a piece of smoked salmon. Mix together the fromage frais and dill with a little freshly ground black pepper and dollop on top of the blinis. Spoon over a little of the mock caviar (if using) and add a sprig of dill for garnish. Serve immediately.

Mini Filo Pastries

Total **POINTS** values per recipe **9** ✤ Calories per serving **76** ✤ Takes 15 minutes to prepare, 15 minutes to cook ✤ Serves **8** (2 each) ♥

You could make these canapés ahead of time and warm through in the oven before serving.

low fat cooking spray
1 large carrot, peeled and diced
2 banana shallots or 4 round shallots, chopped finely
1 large red or green pepper, de-seeded and diced
4 x 15 g sheets filo pastry
6 x 30 g (1¼ oz) sun-dried tomatoes, reconstituted according to the packet instructions
2 tablespoons sun-dried tomato paste
60 g (2 oz) light soft mozzarella, cut into chunks

1 Preheat the oven to Gas Mark 6/200°C/fan oven 180°C. Spray a non stick frying pan with low fat cooking spray and heat until hot. Add the carrot, shallots and pepper and cook for 5 minutes until softened. Add a little water if the mixture gets too dry.

2 Spray each sheet of filo pastry with low fat cooking spray and cut each sheet into eight rectangles. In a 16 hole non stick mini muffin tin (see tip), place two layered rectangles at an angle in each hole. Press down gently to the bottom.

3 Cut the soaked tomatoes into thin strips and stir into the carrot mixture with the sun-dried tomato paste. Fill the pastry cases with the mixture and top each with a piece of mozzarella. Bake for 12–15 minutes until golden. Serve warm.

Tip If you don't have a mini muffin tin, place the filo rectangles in small cake papers in a bun tin to bake.

Quorn and Nut Roast with Tomato Sauce

2½ POINTS VALUE

Total **POINTS** values per recipe **16** + Calories per serving **201** + Takes 25 minutes to prepare, 30 minutes to cook + Serves **6** ♥ ❄

This can be made ahead and frozen.

low fat cooking spray
1 large onion, chopped
1 garlic clove, crushed
1 x 300 g packet frozen Quorn mince
110 g (4 oz) fresh brown breadcrumbs
60 g (2 oz) mixed chopped nuts
1 tablespoon mixed dried herbs
1 tablespoon yeast extract, dissolved in
  2 tablespoons hot water
1 egg, beaten
2 tomatoes, sliced
2 teaspoons poppy seeds

For the sauce:
1 x 400 g can chopped tomatoes
½ vegetable stock cube, crumbled
1 tablespoon tomato purée

1 Preheat the oven to Gas Mark 4/180°C/fan oven 160°C. Line a 900 g (2 lb) loaf tin with non stick baking parchment.

2 Spray a small non stick frying pan with low fat cooking spray, add the onion and cook for 10 minutes over a low heat until softened. Add the garlic and cook for a further minute.

3 Place the Quorn, breadcrumbs, nuts and herbs in a large bowl, mix well and stir in the onion and garlic. Add the yeast extract and egg and mix to a thick batter consistency with 300 ml (10 fl oz) water. Spoon half the mixture into the tin, top with the tomato slices and then add the remaining mixture. Sprinkle with the poppy seeds and bake for 30 minutes until brown on the top and set.

4 For the sauce, place the ingredients in a small pan, bring to the boil and simmer for 2–3 minutes until hot and slightly thickened. Serve the nut roast sliced, with the sauce drizzled over.

Beef Bourguignon

4½ POINTS VALUE

Total **POINTS** values per recipe **18** + Calories per serving **271** + Takes 25 minutes to prepare, 2 hours to cook + Serves **4** ❄

Make this stew the day before and let the flavours mingle and develop. It is a great dish for Boxing Day when you've had enough of turkey.

500 g (1 lb 2 oz) lean braising beef, cut into chunks
low fat cooking spray
4 shallots, halved
1 celery stick, chopped
2 garlic cloves, chopped
175 g (6 oz) large field mushrooms, quartered
2 tablespoons flour
300 ml (10 fl oz) red wine
150 ml (5 fl oz) hot beef stock
1 bay leaf
2 tablespoons chopped fresh parsley, to garnish

1 Preheat the oven to Gas Mark 3/160°C/fan oven 140°C. Heat a large lidded, ovenproof pan until hot. Spray the beef with low fat cooking spray and place in the pan. Cook for 3–5 minutes stirring occasionally until brown all over. You may need to do this in batches. Remove the beef from the pan and set aside. Spray the pan, add the shallots and celery and stir fry for 3 minutes before adding the garlic. Cook for another 2 minutes until the vegetables are softened. Add the mushrooms and cook over a medium heat for 5 minutes before returning the beef to the pan. Stir in the flour and cook for 1 minute.

2 Add the wine, stock and bay leaf and bring to the boil. Cover and cook in the oven for 2 hours.

3 Remove the bay leaf from the dish and serve the casserole garnished with parsley.

Serving suggestion Serve with mashed potato made with 450 g (1 lb) floury potatoes, boiled and mashed, with 3 tablespoons of skimmed milk and a little seasoning and steamed green beans, for an extra 1½ **POINTS** values per serving.

4½ POINTS VALUE

Roast Beef with Mustard Crust

Total *POINTS* values per recipe **43** + Calories per serving **316**
+ Takes 40 minutes to prepare, 40 minutes to cook +
Serves **6**

A lean version of the traditional Sunday
beef with all the trimmings and a
mustard topping.

For the roast potatoes:
low fat cooking spray
600 g (1 lb 5 oz) potatoes, peeled and cut into large
   chunks
8 garlic cloves, unpeeled

For the Yorkshire puddings:
125 g (4½ oz) plain flour
1 egg
100 ml (3½ fl oz) skimmed milk mixed with 100 ml
   (3½ fl oz) water

For the beef:
650 g (1 lb 8 oz) top rump/topside joint
2 tablespoons wholegrain mustard
1 teaspoon English mustard

To serve:
4 heaped teaspoons (14 g total weight) beef gravy
   granules
300 ml (10 fl oz) boiling water

1 Preheat the oven to Gas Mark 7/220°C/fan oven
200°C. Spray a roasting tin with low fat cooking
spray and heat in the oven for 5–10 minutes until
hot. Meanwhile, bring a pan of water to the boil, add
the potatoes, return to the boil and simmer for 5
minutes. Drain thoroughly. Remove the roasting tin
from the oven, carefully add the potatoes with the
garlic cloves, spray with low fat cooking spray and
return to the oven for 30–40 minutes (see tip).

2 For the Yorkshire puddings, put the flour in a
bowl and make a well in the centre. Add the
egg and begin stirring to draw in the flour. When it
is too stiff to stir, gradually add the milk and water
mixture a little at a time until you get a smooth batter.
Alternatively, place all the batter ingredients in a food
processor and blend until smooth. Transfer to a jug
and set aside.

3 Place the beef in a small roasting tin. Mix
together the two mustards and smear all over
the beef. Roast the beef above the potatoes for 15
minutes, then reduce the temperature to Gas Mark
2/150°C/fan oven 130°C and roast the beef for a
further 25 minutes for medium rare.

4 Remove the beef from the oven, cover with foil
and leave to rest whilst cooking the Yorkshire
puddings. Leave the potatoes in the oven to continue
cooking.

5 Increase the oven temperature to Gas Mark
7/220°C/fan oven 200°C. Spray a 12 hole bun tin
with low fat cooking spray, place in the oven for 3–4
minutes and heat until hot. Working quickly, remove
the bun tin from the oven and pour a portion of the
batter into each hole. Return to the oven and cook
at Gas Mark 7/220°C/fan oven 200°C for 15 minutes
until golden and puffed up.

6 Make up the gravy granules with the boiling
water according to the packet instructions.

7 To serve, carve the beef, divide evenly along
with the potatoes between warm plates and
serve with two Yorkshire puddings each and the
gravy poured over.

Tip Sunday lunch is all about timing – make
sure your potatoes go in first and get at least 30
minutes at a high temperature. After that they can
go down to the same temperature as the beef and
remain crispy.

Serving suggestion Serve with steamed
carrots, green beans and broccoli, for no
additional *POINTS* values.

Sweet Sensations

In this chapter you will find a selection of sweet recipes suitable for any festive occasion. Delve into a Christmas Filo Tartlet or try the luscious Lemon Log or the Pavlova with Roasted Vanilla Plums. The recipes are cleverly put together to provide low *POINTS* values along with lots of flavour, so surprise your friends with something sensationally sweet.

Orange and Pumpkin Mousses

Total **POINTS** values per recipe 8½ ✦ Calories per serving 85 ✦ Takes 20 minutes to prepare + cooling + 30 minutes chilling ✦ Serves 4 ♥

Pumpkin is naturally sweet and great at taking on other flavours such as spices.

110 g (4 oz) pumpkin or butternut squash, peeled, de-seeded and chopped
1 cinnamon stick, broken in half
2 oranges, with finely grated zest from 1
2 tablespoons artificial sweetener
400 g (14 oz) low fat natural fromage frais

1 Place the pumpkin or squash in a lidded pan with the cinnamon stick and 4 tablespoons of water. Bring to the boil, cover and simmer for 10 minutes until soft. Remove the cinnamon stick, drain thoroughly and mash.

2 Cut the skin from both the oranges and segment, collecting any juices from the segments.

3 Stir the orange zest and sweetener into the mashed pumpkin with any juices from the orange. Set aside to cool completely.

4 Once cool, fold in the fromage frais and spoon into serving glasses. Chill for 30 minutes before serving. Decorate with the orange segments.

Variation If you have ground cinnamon to hand, flavour the cooked and mashed pumpkin with 1 teaspoon instead of cooking it with the cinnamon stick, for the same **POINTS** values.

Spicy Nectarines

Total **POINTS** values per recipe 7½ ✦ Calories per serving 86 ✦ Takes 15 minutes ✦ Serves 4 ♥ ❄ (fruit only)

Poaching fruit is often a great way to use any excess. It will keep in the fridge or you could freeze it.

6 nectarines or peaches, halved and stoned
1 star anise
2 tablespoons artificial sweetener, plus 2 teaspoons
4 tablespoons low fat natural fromage frais
1 teaspoon mixed spice

1 Place the nectarines or peaches in a lidded saucepan with the star anise, 2 tablespoons sweetener and 150 ml (5 fl oz) water. Bring to the boil, cover and simmer for 10 minutes or until softened. Remove from the heat and cool slightly.

2 Mix the 2 teaspoons of sweetener into the fromage frais with the mixed spice. Serve the warm fruit and its juices with a dollop of spiced fromage frais.

Tip Cool, cover and refridgerate the fruit for up to 3 days.

Cinnamon Pear Custards

Total **POINTS** values per recipe **14** + Calories per serving **110**
+ Takes 10 minutes to prepare, 30 minutes to cook + cooling +
2 hours chilling + Serves **8** ✓

Light creamy custards, which come baked
with cinnamon, lemon and pears.

4 ripe pears, peeled, cored and sliced
4 eggs, beaten
150 g (5½ oz) low fat soft cheese
3 tablespoons artificial sweetener
300 ml (10 fl oz) skimmed milk
finely grated zest of 2 lemons
2 teaspoons cinnamon, for dusting

1 Preheat the oven to Gas Mark 3/160°C/fan oven
140°C. Place eight ramekins in a roasting tin.
Put the pear slices in the bottom of the ramekins so
that their ends stick up.

2 In a jug, beat together the eggs, soft cheese
and sweetener, then stir in the milk and lemon
zest. Pour over the pears (the pears should stick out
of the custard). Fill the roasting tin with hot water so
that it comes halfway up the side of the ramekins.
Bake for 30 minutes until the custards are just set
but slightly wobbly. Remove the ramekins from the
tin and set aside to cool before chilling for at least 2
hours. Dust with cinnamon before serving.

Tip If preferred, you could serve these custards
warm from the oven.

Mango and Passion Fruit Mousses

Total **POINTS** values per recipe **18** + Calories per serving **116**
+ Takes 15 minutes + Serves **8** ✓

A light and tangy mousse with the added
crunch of passion fruit seeds.

3 large ripe mangos
300 g (10½ oz) low fat soft cheese
3–4 teaspoons artificial sweetener
3 egg whites
6 passion fruit, halved

1 Cut down the sides of the stone of the mangoes
and then cut off the skin. Remove any more
flesh that you can from the stones before discarding
them. Roughly chop the flesh and place in a food
processor or use a hand blender. Blend to a purée.
Add the soft cheese and sweetener to taste and
blend again.

2 In a clean grease-free bowl, whisk the egg
whites until they hold stiff peaks. Place the
mango mix in a bowl and carefully fold in the
egg whites.

3 Scoop the flesh and seeds from the passion
fruit. Using eight serving glasses, layer the
mango mix with a spoonful of passion fruit. Repeat,
ending with the passion fruit. Serve immediately.

Tip Try to buy ripe mangos – not too firm but
with a bit of give to the flesh, as they have a
better flavour and are naturally sweeter.

Christmas Fruit Salad

Total **POINTS** values per recipe **8½** ✛ Calories per serving **79** ✛ Takes 15 minutes to prepare + 30 minutes chilling ✛ Serves **8** ✔

Lychees are a great Christmas treat available fresh in most supermarkets at this time of year.

600 g (1 lb 5 oz) lychees, peeled, halved and stoned
6 mandarins or seedless clementines, peeled and segmented
275 g (9½ oz) seedless red grapes, halved
finely grated zest and segments of 2 oranges
4 teaspoons freshly grated ginger
2 teaspoons artificial sweetener

1 Mix together the lychees, mandarins and grapes and place in a serving bowl.

2 Cut away the skin from the oranges. Segment by cutting between the segments, collecting any juice as you work. Add the segments to the salad and place the juice in a small pan with the zest, ginger, sweetener and 4 tablespoons of water. Bring to the boil and simmer for 1 minute. Pour over the fruit and leave to infuse for 5 minutes before chilling for 30 minutes.

Variation Cherries are often around at Christmas, so try substituting the grapes with 40 halved and stoned cherries, for the same **POINTS** values.

Christmas Filo Tartlets

Total **POINTS** values per recipe **10½** ✛ Calories per serving **91** ✛ Takes 15 minutes to prepare, 20–25 minutes to cook + cooling ✛ Serves **8** ✔ (if using vegetarian mincemeat)

Grated apple is added to the mincemeat, making it lighter and less rich, as well as reducing the **POINTS** values.

4 x 15 g sheets filo pastry, each cut into six squares
15 g (½ oz) low fat polyunsaturated margarine, melted
150 g (5½ oz) mincemeat
1 large eating apple, peeled and cored
1 teaspoon icing sugar, to dust

1 Preheat the oven to Gas Mark 5/190°C/fan oven 170°C. Brush each square of filo with the melted margarine and place one square in the base of a hole of a 12 hole non stick bun tin. Layer with another two squares at angles and then repeat to make eight tartlet cases.

2 Place the mincemeat in a bowl and grate in the apple before mixing well. Place a spoonful of mixture into each hole and gently press down the filo corners, leaving the middle exposed. Bake for 20–25 minutes until the pastry is golden. Cool in the tin before dusting with icing sugar and serving warm.

Tip Store in an airtight container for up to 2 days.

Lemon Log

(3½ POINTS VALUE)

Total **POINTS** values per recipe **22½** ⊹ Calories per serving **224** ⊹ Takes 10 minutes to prepare + 1 hour chilling ⊹ Serves **6** ⓥ

This is a lovely lemon version of tiramisu. You can make it up to 4 hours ahead of time to allow all the ingredients to soak together, so it is great for entertaining.

225 g (8 oz) 0% fat Greek yogurt
100 g (3½ oz) low fat soft cheese
5 tablespoons lemon curd
1½ tablespoons icing sugar, sifted
18 sponge fingers (total weight 150 g/5½ oz)
4–5 tablespoons lemon flavoured liqueur
strips of lemon zest, to decorate

1 Mix together the yogurt, soft cheese, lemon curd and icing sugar.

2 Briefly dip the sponge fingers into the lemon liqueur, then arrange a row of six on a serving plate. Spread a third of the yogurt mixture over the sponge fingers. Repeat, ending with the yogurt mixture. Drizzle any remaining strips of lemon liqueur over the top.

3 Chill for at least an hour before slicing and serve decorated with the strips of lemon zest.

Variation Make an orange version of this with orange curd, an orange liqueur and strips of orange zest to decorate. The **POINTS** values will be 4 per serving.

Apple and Pear Filo Tarte Tatin

(1½ POINTS VALUE)

Total **POINTS** values per recipe **9½** ⊹ Calories per serving **101** ⊹ Takes 15 minutes to prepare, 25 minutes to cook ⊹ Serves **6** ⓥ

The fruit and brown sugar caramelise deliciously around the edges of this upside down tart.

4 tablespoons brown sugar
25 g (1 oz) low fat polyunsaturated margarine, melted
finely grated zest and juice of a small lemon
200 g (7 oz) Bramley apples, peeled, cored and sliced
150 g (5½ oz) pears, peeled, cored and sliced
4 x 15 g sheets filo pastry

1 Place the sugar, half the margarine, lemon zest and juice in a non stick frying pan and heat until hot. Add the apple and pear slices, stir to coat and cook for 3–4 minutes until just softened.

2 Preheat the oven to Gas Mark 6/200°C/fan oven 180°C. Base line a 20 cm (8 inch) round baking tin with non stick baking parchment. Spoon the fruit and juices into the tin. Brush a sheet of filo pastry with some of the remaining melted margarine and place on top of the fruit, tucking the edges down the sides. Repeat, brushing and layering the remaining pastry sheets so they cover the fruit completely. Bake for 20 minutes until golden.

3 To serve, loosen the edges round the tin, place a plate on top and invert to tip it out. Remove the baking parchment and serve in wedges.

Variation Try the recipe with the zest and juice of an orange or ½ teaspoon cinnamon added to the fruit instead of the lemon, for no additional **POINTS** values.

Serving suggestion Serve with a 60 g (2 oz) scoop of low fat ice cream per person, for an additional **POINTS** value of 1 per serving.

Pavlova with Roasted Vanilla Plums

(4 POINTS VALUE)

Total *POINTS* values per recipe 33½ ✛ Calories per serving **192** ✛ Takes 15 minutes to prepare, 1 hour to cook + chilling ✛ Serves **8** ✓

Plums and a little spice make this a great autumn or winter pudding.

For the meringue:
3 egg whites
175 g (6 oz) caster sugar

For the filling:
750 g (1 lb 10 oz) plums, halved and stoned
3 tablespoons light brown sugar
1 vanilla pod, slit lengthways

To serve:
150 ml (5 fl oz) low fat whipping cream such as Elmlea
1 x 150 g pot 0% fat Greek yogurt

1 Preheat the oven to Gas Mark 2/150°C/fan oven 130°C. Line a baking tray with non stick baking parchment. Whisk the egg whites in a clean bowl until they hold stiff peaks. Whisk in half the caster sugar until the mixture is thick and glossy and then carefully fold in the remainder. Spread the mixture on the baking parchment to form a circle approximately 20 cm (8 inch) in diameter. Make a slight dip in the middle to hold the filling. Bake for 1 hour until the meringue feels dry. Remove from the oven and, keeping it on the paper, cool on a wire rack.

2 Meanwhile, place the plums in an ovenproof dish, sprinkle over the brown sugar and drizzle with 150 ml (5 fl oz) water. Tuck the vanilla pod under the plums. Bake at the same temperature as the meringue for 1 hour until soft and juicy. Remove from the oven. Take out the vanilla pod and scrape out the seeds. Discard the pod and stir the seeds into the plum juices. Cool and then chill.

3 To serve, slide the meringue on to a plate. Whip the cream until it holds soft peaks then fold in the yogurt. Spoon the mixture on to the meringue, top with the plums and drizzle over a bit of the sauce.

Pumpkin Pie

(5 POINTS VALUE)

Total *POINTS* values per recipe 29½ ✛ Calories per serving **264** ✛ Takes 25 minutes to prepare, 30 minutes to cook ✛ Serves **6** ✓

Once you have made this pie you won't want to keep this as a Halloween special – the spice and creaminess of the cheese make it a delicious dessert for any time of year.

1 x 230 g large unbaked shortcrust pastry case such as Saxbys
350 g (12 oz) pumpkin or butternut squash, peeled, de-seeded and diced
50 g (1¾ oz) brown sugar
1½ tablespoons mixed spice
2 eggs, beaten
75 g (2¾ oz) low fat soft cheese
½ teaspoon cinnamon, for dusting

1 Preheat the oven to Gas Mark 6/200°C/fan oven180°C. Keeping the pastry in its foil case, blind bake by pricking the base and cooking without any filling for 10–15 minutes until just golden. Remove from the oven.

2 Meanwhile, place the pumpkin (or squash) in a lidded pan with 150 ml (5 fl oz) water, cover and cook for 10 minutes until soft. Drain well and mash.

3 Add the sugar and spice to the pumpkin. Leave to cool slightly before beating in the eggs and soft cheese. Sieve the mixture to remove any stringy bits of pumpkin and pour into the pastry case. Don't worry if the mixture looks thin, it will thicken and set in the oven. Bake for 30 minutes until the filling has set and the pastry is a deep golden colour. Leave in the foil container for 5 minutes before serving warm, dusted with the cinnamon.

Tip Unbaked pastry cases are available in most supermarkets in the butter and margarine section.

Tip If you can't find a pastry case, make your own using 250 g (9 oz) ready made shortcrust pastry in a 20 cm (8 inch) diameter tin, for a *POINTS* value of 5½ per serving.

5
POINTS
VALUE

Mocha Chestnut Tart

Total *POINTS* values per recipe **36½** + Calories per serving **173** + Takes 20 minutes to prepare, 30 minutes to cook + 10 minutes cooling + chilling + Serves **10** ♥

Chestnut purée is a slightly sweet, smooth paste that is found in cans, usually amongst the stuffing ingredients in supermarkets. It is useful for cooking as it low in *POINTS* values.

150 g (5½ oz) plain chocolate, broken into squares
75 g (2¾ oz) low fat polyunsaturated margarine
4 tablespoons strong black coffee, cooled
200 g (7 oz) chestnut purée
60 g (2 oz) caster sugar
2 eggs, separated, plus 2 egg whites
1 teaspoon cocoa, for dusting

1   Preheat the oven to Gas Mark 5/190°C/fan oven 170°C. Line the base of a 20 cm (8 inch) springform tin with non stick baking parchment.

2   Place the chocolate, margarine and coffee in a non metallic bowl and microwave on high for 1 minute. Stir and repeat in 30 second blasts until the chocolate has melted. Mix well. Alternatively, place the bowl over a pan of simmering water, being careful that the water does not touch the bottom of the bowl, and stir gently until the chocolate has melted.

3   Beat the chestnut purée in a bowl until smooth, then beat in the sugar and egg yolks. Stir in the chocolate mixture to form a smooth paste.

4   In a clean, grease-free bowl, whisk all the egg whites until they hold stiff peaks. Carefully fold into the chocolate mixture. Spoon into the tin and bake for 30 minutes until firm. Cool in the tin for 10 minutes, then chill completely before serving dusted with the cocoa.

Serving suggestion Serve this with a 60 g (2 oz) scoop of low fat ice cream per person, for an extra 1 *POINTS* value per serving.

Index by *POINTS* values

Index